A SILENT THUNDER

Eduardo Iván López

BROADWAY PLAY PUBLISHING INC
224 E 62nd St, NY NY 10065-8201
212 772-8334 fax: 212 772-8358
BroadwayPlayPub.com

A SILENT THUNDER
© 1995 by Eduardo Iván López

All rights reserved. This work is fully protected under the copyright laws of the United States of America. No part of this publication may be photocopied, reproduced, stored in a retrieval system, or transmitted, in any form or by any means, electronic, mechanical, recording, or otherwise, without the prior permission of the publisher. Additional copies of this play are available from the publisher.

Written permission is required for live performance of any sort. This includes readings, cuttings, scenes, and excerpts. For amateur and stock performances, please contact Broadway Play Publishing Inc. For all other rights please contact the author c/o B P P I.

Cover photo by Austin Trevett

I S B N: 978-0-88145-116-0

First printing: May 1995
This printing: September 2016

Book design: Marie Donovan
Page make-up: Adobe Indesign
Typeface: Palatino

A SILENT THUNDER was originally produced by the Apple Corps Theater, N Y N Y (John Raymond and Michael Tolan, Artistic Directors), opening on 26 June 1990. The cast and creative contributors were:

JOE SANTANA .... Nestor Carbonell
KIMIYO ....Suzen Murakoshi

Director .... John Cappelletti
Set design .... Randy Benjamin
Lighting design .... William J Plachy
Costume design .... Maryann D Smith
Sound design .... Neal Arluck
Production stage manager .... Ken Simmons

CHARACTERS & SETTING

JOE SANTANA, *a young Marine corporal in his early twenties*

KIMIYO, *a young Okinawan woman of eighteen*

The time: The spring of 1966

The place: Kadena, Okinawa, the largest of the Ryukyu Islands in the west Pacific, southwest of Japan. Taken by U S forces in World War II, at the time of the play it is under U S military administration.

ACT ONE

Scene One: *A tailor shop, early evening*

Scene Two: *A hotel room in a small, native hotel, later that night*

ACT TWO

Scene One: *The same hotel room, late evening, early morning*

Scene Two: *The same hotel room, later that night*

Scene Three: *The same hotel room, early morning the next day*

THE SET

The play has two settings: a small tailor shop and a hotel room. Both are in the town of Kadena, Okinawa.

The tailor shop suggested here is small and intimate with just a few furniture pieces such as a service counter, a portable full-length mirror, a clothes rack on rollers, and a mannequin.

The shop is downstage of the hotel room and separated from it by a roll-down bamboo curtain, which hides the back set from view. The outside door of the tailor shop is upstage left, next to the bamboo curtain, and leads into a fenced courtyard.

The removal of most of the tailor shop furniture at the end of Scene One should be incorporated into SANTANA's action as he helps KIMIYO close up the shop for the night.

During the blackout between scenes, the bamboo curtain is rolled up (out of sight), exposing the interior of the hotel room.

The hotel room is comfortable, with its walls and floor composed of light, natural wood. There is an outside door stage center right, a window with a shade overlooking a tree full of cherry blossoms on the back wall, a sink with an enameled wash pan, a wash rack with towels, a rectangular table that stands close to the floor, and a double bed covered with a pastel quilt.

This play is dedicated to the leading ladies in my life:

Mamita (Julie) who gave me life and ambition

my sisters Grace and Celeste, who gave me support when I most needed it

my daughter Elizabeth (Sherry),
who has been a constant source of joy for me since she made her debut in my life

and my best friend and wife, Roma,
whose unwavering love has made it all possible

ACT ONE

Scene One

(At rise: KIMIYO, *an Asian girl of eighteen with shoulder-length hair and bangs that form a straight line across her forehead, stands in front of the mannequin, which is wearing a men's grey suit jacket. She wears the navy blue uniform of a school girl. She is the center of attraction at a grand ball, and the suit jacket is her imaginary Prince Charming. She holds the sleeve of the jacket as she speaks.)*

KIMIYO: *(Coquettishly)* My goodness, Sir. I do not know what to say. You take my bleath away... Dance? Why I hadly know you. Well, I suppose one dance, but just one. I must be fair to the other gentlemen. *(She takes the jacket and begins dancing with it. She laughs as she dances.)* You are so charming, Sir... What, run away with you? But what of my family? —Oh, well, pelhaps after tea.

*(*KIMIYO *giggles and continues her dance.* SANTANA, *a cocky, early-twenties Marine wearing dress greens with a chest full of ribbons, enters. Unaware of his presence, she continues to dance. He watches her with amusement.)*

SANTANA: Hai sai.

*(*KIMIYO *jumps at the sound of* SANTANA's *voice and quickly covers her face in embarrassment.)*

SANTANA: Where big honcho, baby-san?

*(*KIMIYO *shrugs.)*

SANTANA: Is he coming back soon?

(KIMIYO *shakes her head.*)

SANTANA: Well, I gotta have my suit. Can you get it for me? The name is Santana.

KIMIYO: Kimiyo know.

(*Totally embarrassed,* KIMIYO *hands* SANTANA *the suit jacket in her hands.*)

SANTANA: Hey, you've been dancing with my suit. How did I do? Did I step on your toes?

(KIMIYO *covers her face in shame.*)

SANTANA: Oh, c'mon, baby-san. I'm only teasing. Can I try it on?

(KIMIYO *nods with her face still covered.* SANTANA *stands in front of the mirror. He looks back and catches her sneaking a look. She quickly covers her face again. He holds out the jacket to her.*)

SANTANA: C'mon. Give me a hand with this thing.

(KIMIYO *takes the jacket and, with a bowed head, holds it while* SANTANA *slips into it.*)

KIMIYO: You like?

SANTANA: I'm not sure. What do you think?

(KIMIYO *blushes.*)

SANTANA: That bad, huh?

KIMIYO: Oh, no!...

SANTANA: (*Looking around*) Boss-man did a good job. When is he coming back?

KIMIYO: Not come. Tomorrow. He tomorrow come, yes?

SANTANA: No. Watashi no can come back tomorrow. Must take suit now. Watashi pay you money. You give honcho-san.

ACT ONE 3

KIMIYO: Kimiyo not know price.

SANTANA: Santana knows. Thirty-five dollars. I buy long time ago. Two months. But watashi no can pay. Always broke. But now Santana have money. Pay for suit. Make boss-man very, very happy.

KIMIYO: I know. I know G I. Come eight weeks buy suit.

SANTANA: You know me?

KIMIYO: Yes. Kimiyo help uncle make suit. Stand on chair, measure Santana-san.

SANTANA: Yeah?...I'm beginning to remember... But you look different somehow.

KIMIYO: Hair grow long now.

SANTANA: That's it. It was shorter.

KIMIYO: School master not let pupil hair grow. Must all cut hair same.

SANTANA: Hmn. It looks better this way.

KIMIYO: *(Surprised)* You like?

SANTANA: Kimiyo not baby-san no more. Now big, good-looking naisan. Have plenty nisans chasing after her.

KIMIYO: Oh, no! School pupil not have honeywa. Big— how you say—taboo. No can have boyfriend.

SANTANA: Why not?

KIMIYO: Too young. Must finish school first.

SANTANA: Yeah. But don't you cheat a little bit, huh? Go in woods once in a while with nisan?

KIMIYO: No! Nisan not look baby-san. All school pupil baby-san until school finish. That's why uniform wear.

SANTANA: Yeah? You mean all you girls wearing uniforms can't horse around until you finish school?

KIMIYO: What "horse around" mean?

SANTANA: Hanky panky, you know.

KIMIYO: Hanky panky?

SANTANA: Boy want to make waku-waku with baby-san.

(KIMIYO *blushes*.)

KIMIYO: Not can do. Taboo!

SANTANA: You never make waku-waku?

KIMIYO: No! No!

SANTANA: Too bad, baby-san. You're missing a lot of fun. *(He pulls out some bills.)* Look, I'm gonna take the suit now 'cause I won't have any time in the morning before I leave.

KIMIYO: Santana-san go?

SANTANA: Yeah. Take big ship tomorrow night and go very, very far.

KIMIYO: Not come back?

SANTANA: I don't know. Not for a long time anyway.

KIMIYO: Santana-san not like Okinawa?

SANTANA: Sure, I like. But when Uncle Sam say go, Santana-san must go.

KIMIYO: Oh.

SANTANA: *(Giving her money)* Here's thirty-five dollars. Give it to boss-man, okay?

KIMIYO: Okay. I put suit in bag. *(She takes the suit to the counter and slips a plastic bag over it.)*

SANTANA: Not too busy, huh?

KIMIYO: Nobody come. I go home now.

SANTANA: You mean you gotta close up by yourself?

KIMIYO: I can do.

ACT ONE

SANTANA: You want me to help you?

KIMIYO: No, no. Kimiyo do.

SANTANA: You finish checking me out. I'll have you out of here in no time.

(SANTANA *pushes the mannequin, the mirror, and the clothes rack to the side while* KIMIYO *does the paper work. She hands him the suit.)*

SANTANA: Which way you walking?

KIMIYO: To corner. Take bus to Naha.

SANTANA: Naha? That's twenty miles. You travel that every day?

KIMIYO: I take bus. Not so bad.

SANTANA: What time does your bus leave?

KIMIYO: Forty and five minutes.

SANTANA: Forty-five minutes? That's a long time. C'mon. I'll buy you a cup of tea.

KIMIYO: Tea?

SANTANA: Yeah. While you wait for the bus.

KIMIYO: You take Kimiyo?

SANTANA: Why, is it taboo?

KIMIYO: Yes. Big, big taboo. Kimiyo no can do.

SANTANA: You're sure?

KIMIYO: Kimiyo very, very sure.

SANTANA: In that case, thank your uncle for me and have a nice trip to Naha.

KIMIYO: You go?

SANTANA: Yeah.

KIMIYO: Where you go?

SANTANA: Back to the base.

(KIMIYO *thinks quickly.*)

KIMIYO: *(Resolutely)* No can have tea here. Go far. Kimiyo can have tea long way up street where uncle friends no can see.

SANTANA: Where?

KIMIYO: You go, Kimiyo follow.

SANTANA: Are you sure you want to do this? I don't want to get you in trouble.

KIMIYO: You walk far ahead. I stay back. Nobody see Kimiyo, not get into trouble.

SANTANA: Don't stay too far back, or you'll lose me.

KIMIYO: Kimiyo not lose. I haiako after Santana-san. Now we go, yes?

SANTANA: If you think it's okay.

(KIMIYO *shoos him out with her hands.*)

KIMIYO: We go.

(SANTANA *exits.* KIMIYO *waits a moment and then follows him.*)

(*The lights fade to black.*)

(*End of scene*)

Scene Two

(*Lights up on a hotel room. The room is empty. After a moment,* SANTANA *opens the door and enters. A late afternoon light comes through the window, illuminating the tree with its blossoms and casting a warm glow in the room.*)

(SANTANA *slips out of his jacket and hangs it up neatly on a coat hanger hanging from a hook on the door. He checks himself in the mirror and removes his tie. He tests the springs on the bed, sits, lights up a cigarette, and waits.*)

ACT ONE

(There is a soft knock on the door. SANTANA *opens it and finds* KIMIYO *meekly standing there. He takes her hand and leads her into the room. As soon as she's in, she bursts into tears.)*

SANTANA: What's the matter? What happened?

*(*KIMIYO *throws herself on the bed sobbing.)*

SANTANA: Why are you crying?

KIMIYO: Kimiyo do something bad, very, very bad. Not should come to hotel room. Only number four geisha come to hotel with G I. Kimiyo lose face.

SANTANA: Now wait a minute. The only reason I came in here was because you wouldn't go into any of the tea houses. Every time I'd go into a place and sit at a table, you'd stand outside and wave no to me. What was I supposed to do? We've been walking for over an hour. I didn't know where else to go. I figured, if you were so afraid of being seen, a hotel room was the perfect place.

KIMIYO: Now Kimiyo like geisha person. Bad, bad woman.

SANTANA: Look, nothing is gonna happen here. Your reputation is safe. I told the guy downstairs to bring us some tea and sake. If you're hungry, I'll ask him to bring us some food.

KIMIYO: Hotel man see Kimiyo. Kimiyo die now.

SANTANA: What do you mean he saw you? He doesn't know who you are.

KIMIYO: He see uniform. He know me school pupil. Now he see me with G I. That bad, very, very bad.

SANTANA: Will you cut it out already? You're still the same girl you were an hour ago. We haven't done a damn thing.

KIMIYO: Kimiyo missed bus. No can go home now.

SANTANA: You'll take the next bus.

KIMIYO: Tomorrow bus come.

SANTANA: Tomorrow? You mean there are no more buses tonight?

KIMIYO: No.

SANTANA: Oh, shit!... No sweat. I'll put you in a cab. The cab will take you right to your front door. It's even better than a bus.

KIMIYO: Mama-san wait for Kimiyo at bus stop. When she no see me on bus, she know Kimiyo miss bus. Then she know.

SANTANA: All right. Let's forget the tea. We'll go downstairs and I'll put you in a taxi. If you leave now, the taxi will get to Naha before the bus, and nobody will be the wiser. You can hide until the bus gets there, and then you can meet your mother. How's that?

KIMIYO: She no see me come from bus.

SANTANA: Tell her you made a mistake and got off at the wrong stop. I'm sure you can work it out. Now stop crying and go wash your face.

KIMIYO: I no can tell lie. Mama-san will know.

SANTANA: Look, you can lie if you have to. Believe me. You can lie.

KIMIYO: I no can go home now. I lose face.

SANTANA: Damn it, Kimiyo. If you had just gone into one of those tea houses, you wouldn't have missed the bus, and none of this would've happened.

(KIMIYO *starts to cry again.*)

SANTANA: Oh, Christ! What do you wanna do here?

KIMIYO: I, I go. Walk home.

ACT ONE

SANTANA: Are you crazy? Twenty miles? C'mon. I'll put you in a cab.

KIMIYO: Santana-san not want Kimiyo?

SANTANA: We gotta get you out of here before that bus gets to Naha.

KIMIYO: Too late. Kimiyo not can go home now.

SANTANA: It's not too late. Now, c'mon. Every minute we lose is gonna be tough to make up.

KIMIYO: I not have money.

SANTANA: I've got money. Now let's go.

(KIMIYO *sniffles.*)

SANTANA: What in the hell are you crying about now?

KIMIYO: I not want to go home.

(SANTANA *eyes* KIMIYO *suspiciously.*)

SANTANA: What did you say?

KIMIYO: *(Determinedly)* I want to have tea.

SANTANA: What about mama-san and your reputation?

KIMIYO: Too late.

SANTANA: Hey, you're not pulling my leg with this mama-san business, are you?

KIMIYO: Pulling leg?

SANTANA: Never mind.

KIMIYO: I stay here.

SANTANA: Here?

KIMIYO: Hotel room. Can Kimiyo stay hotel room?

SANTANA: Why do you wanna stay here?

KIMIYO: Can stay?

SANTANA: Well,...I guess so. But what about tomorrow? This room is only good until noon. What are you going to do after that?

KIMIYO: I not know.

SANTANA: Well, I do. You're gonna be in worse trouble than you are now. No matter how bad you think it's gonna be, you're better off facing the music tonight.

KIMIYO: Face music?

SANTANA: Yeah. It means, you're better off facing mama-san tonight. 'Cause if you put it off 'til tomorrow, you're gonna be in big, big trouble. Mama-san will really be pissed off.

KIMIYO: Piss off?

SANTANA: Never mind. Just go.

KIMIYO: Kimiyo go if Santana-san not want Kimiyo stay.

SANTANA: Hey, your family comes first. If you think they're gonna kick you out, go home. Talk to them. Straighten things out. You'll thank me in the morning.

(KIMIYO *bows her head humbly.*)

KIMIYO: Kimiyo go.

SANTANA: You understand what I'm telling you?

KIMIYO: Kimiyo understand.

(KIMIYO *sniffles as she makes her way to the door.*)

SANTANA: I'm doing this for your own good. Here, don't forget this.

(SANTANA *hands* KIMIYO *her bag. She stands by the door with her head bowed.*)

SANTANA: You're gonna see that I'm right. Oh.

(SANTANA *pulls out some bills and shoves them at* KIMIYO. *She sees the bills and begins to cry again.*)

ACT ONE

SANTANA: What now?

KIMIYO: Bad. Bad woman take money.

SANTANA: You need money for the taxi. How else are you gonna get home?

(KIMIYO *continues crying.*)

SANTANA: All right! Never mind. I'll take you downstairs and pay for the cab myself. Now cut it out! Look. (*He sticks the money back into his pocket.*) See? I put it back into my pocket. There's no reason to cry, right?

KIMIYO: (*Trying to stifle her sobs*) I, I no cry for money.

SANTANA: Then why are you crying?

KIMIYO: Because Santana-san not want useless woman. Say go. Not want Kimiyo.

SANTANA: We've already gone over this.

(*There is a knock at the door.* KIMIYO *hides behind the door.*)

SANTANA: Now what?

KIMIYO: Me hide.

SANTANA: From who? It's the guy downstairs with the tea and sake I ordered.

KIMIYO: No! No open the door. Man see Kimiyo.

SANTANA: Don't be ridiculous. He saw you walk up the stairs.

KIMIYO: No let him see.

SANTANA: All right. Look, I'm gonna open the door a crack…

KIMIYO: No!

SANTANA: Just a crack. He won't see a thing. I'll stick my hand out the door and grab the tray.

KIMIYO: He no see?

SANTANA: Relax. Leave it to me.

(SANTANA *opens the door slightly, reaches out, and pulls in a tray. He fishes into his pocket and hands the clerk some money.*)

SANTANA: *(To the unseen clerk outside the door.)* Arigato gozaimus. *(To* KIMIYO *)* See? Now go wash your face.

(KIMIYO *washes her face.)*

KIMIYO: Santana-san think Kimiyo a foolish children.

SANTANA: Child. Foolish child. Not children. Children is plural.

KIMIYO: What mean plural?

SANTANA: More than one. (SANTANA *shows her one finger.)* One is child. (SANTANA *puts up two fingers.)* Two is children.

KIMIYO: Then Santana-san think Kimiyo enough foolish for many children.

SANTANA: Come over here and drink this tea before it gets cold.

KIMIYO: You let me stay?

SANTANA: As long as you understand that I have to be out of here by nine tomorrow morning.

KIMIYO: You go to base?

SANTANA: I gotta check in by twelve.

KIMIYO: Ah-so! And what of Kimiyo?

SANTANA: You're good here 'til noon. That's twelve o'clock. The room is good 'til then.

KIMIYO: Ahhh! No can stay!

SANTANA: Why not?

KIMIYO: This is strange place.

SANTANA: Just keep the door locked after I leave. No one is gonna bother you.

ACT ONE

KIMIYO: Kimiyo aflaid be by self.

SANTANA: It's gonna be daylight out. People all over the place. You get dressed, go outside, and then go wherever it is you wanna go.

KIMIYO: Then many persons see Kimiyo come from hotel. *(Tears swell in her eyes. She drags her sleeve across her nose.)*

SANTANA: Gimme a break, will ya? If I don't get back to the base by twelve, my top sergeant, big honcho, will throw Santana-san in the brig, jail, you know? He put Santana-san in a cage like a bird. You want Santana-san in a cage?

KIMIYO: No!

SANTANA: Then stop crying so much. Only baby-sans cry all the time. You're a big girl now. Sexy onnasan.

KIMIYO: Santana-san make fun Kimiyo.

SANTANA: *(Suddenly moved by her)* No-no. Santana no make fun. *(He lifts her face gently and wipes her tears with his thumb.)* Kimiyo is a very...beautiful woman. It's just that—God! I don't know if I'm gonna be able to keep my hands off of you.

KIMIYO: Santana-san angry.

SANTANA: This is crazy!

KIMIYO: Me crazy?

SANTANA: Not you, me!—and you too! We're both crazy. And I should know better.

KIMIYO: Me sorry.

SANTANA: For what? You haven't done anything. C'mon, dry your face and come over here. This tea and sake are gonna be like ice pretty soon.

(KIMIYO dries her face then folds the towel neatly. She goes to the table and stands with her head bowed.)

SANTANA: Sit down.

(KIMIYO *remains standing.*)

SANTANA: What?

KIMIYO: No can sit.

SANTANA: Why not?

KIMIYO: Not good manners to sit with man. It is not respectful.

SANTANA: What?

KIMIYO: It is custom.

SANTANA: Well, it ain't the custom around here, so sit down and drink your tea.

(KIMIYO *hesitates.*)

SANTANA: You wanna make Santana happy, don't you?

(KIMIYO *nods.*)

SANTANA: Then sit.

(KIMIYO *sits timidly.* SANTANA *picks up the teapot. She quickly snatches it from him.*)

KIMIYO: Watashi do.

(KIMIYO *pours* SANTANA *a cup and then pours herself one. They sip their tea in silence.*)

KIMIYO: Santana-san no see Kimiyo forever no more.

SANTANA: You never know. They might send me back here again for more training.

KIMIYO: I know. Not see, no more.

SANTANA: You don't believe me?

KIMIYO: You have honeywah in U S A. No want Okinawa woman.

SANTANA: Hey. This is crazy talk. Drink your tea.

KIMIYO: You have Amelica woman?

ACT ONE

SANTANA: What difference does it make? Come tomorrow night, I'm gone. That's the way it's got to be. So let's not complicate things, huh?

KIMIYO: Have Amelica woman?

SANTANA: Yeah. I've got a whole bunch of them. Taksan.

KIMIYO: You not tell truth.

SANTANA: (SANTANA *studies her.*) How do you know?

KIMIYO: I know.

SANTANA: How?

KIMIYO: You too young have many woman.

SANTANA: Yeah? I'm older than you. A lot older.

KIMIYO: How many old?

SANTANA: Never you mind. I've been places. More places than you've ever heard of.

KIMIYO: Go war?

SANTANA: I've been there.

KIMIYO: I not ask question. Bad manners ask question.

SANTANA: It's okay. I'm twenty-one, an old twenty-one.

KIMIYO: Kimiyo fifteen and three.

SANTANA: Eighteen.

KIMIYO: Eight…

SANTANA: Teen

KIMIYO: Eighteen.

SANTANA: You're old for your age too.

KIMIYO: Kimiyo old?

SANTANA: Physically.

KIMIYO: What phy-si-cal-ly?

SANTANA: Never mind. *(He feels the sake bottle, then pours himself a cup.)* It's cold. There's nothing worse than cold sake.

KIMIYO: What we do now, Santana-san?

SANTANA: *(Avoiding the question)* How's your tea?

KIMIYO: Tea good.

SANTANA: You sure you don't want something to eat?

KIMIYO: Me sure.

(SANTANA tastes the sake and makes a face.)

SANTANA: It loses something when it's cold, doesn't it?

KIMIYO: Not know. Not drink sake.

SANTANA: Wanna sip?

KIMIYO: Ahhh, so! Very, very bad onnanoko drink sake!

SANTANA: No one will know.

KIMIYO: Kimiyo know. Feel very, very terrible. Ooouuu!

SANTANA: All right, all right already! I'm sorry I suggested it. *(He glances at his watch.)* Look, I gotta leave in about nine hours. Why don't you try to catch some sleep.

(KIMIYO stands, bows to SANTANA and goes to the counter for the pan of water. She places the pan at his feet. She starts to undo his shoelaces.)

SANTANA: What are you doing?

KIMIYO: Wash your foot.

SANTANA: Wash what?

(KIMIYO takes a firm grip of SANTNA's foot and removes his shoes.)

SANTANA: I don't need my feet washed.

ACT ONE

KIMIYO: No move. Make floor wet.

(KIMIYO *places* SANTANA's *feet in the water.*)

SANTANA: Anybody ever tell you you'd make a good first sergeant?

KIMIYO: *(Massaging his feet)* What first sergeant?

SANTANA: Big honcho. Bosses everybody around. Just like you.

KIMIYO: *(Giggling)* Santana-san very, very funny.

SANTANA: *(Obviously enjoying her massage)* Hey, this foot business isn't bad. This some kind of custom or something?

KIMIYO: Okasan wash otosan foot.

SANTANA: Feet. Plural. *(He shows her one finger.)* One foot. *(He puts up two fingers.)* Two feet.

KIMIYO: Ahhh! Kimiyo is stupid woman. *(She bows her head.)*

SANTANA: No. Kimiyo very smart. Watashi stupid. Spent long time in Far East and learn nothing. At least Kimiyo speak English. Watashi speaks nothing. Well, almost nothing. I speak some bad Spanish.

KIMIYO: No! Santana-san no stupid. Very, very smart. Big, strong, like Amelica movie star.

SANTANA: Yeah? C'mon. What do you know about movie stars?

KIMIYO: Know much. Lock Hudson, ah, Pour Newman, ah, Steve McQueen.

SANTANA: Hey, you've been watching a few flicks.

KIMIYO: Santana-san much, much pretty, yes?

SANTANA: No. Girls, women are pretty. Men are handsome.

KIMIYO: Santana-san handsome.

SANTANA: You're not so bad yourself.

(KIMIYO *takes one of* SANTANA'*s feet from the pan and begins to dry it with the folded towel.*)

KIMIYO: Santana-san, why you buy suit?

SANTANA: Why? Why do people buy suits?

KIMIYO: People wear suit. I see you many, many times come tailor shop. Always wear Maline uniform. Why you buy civilian suit if not want wear?

SANTANA: Well, Kimiyo, I'll tell you a little secret. Whenever I'm stationed anywhere for any length of time, I always order a suit. It gives me something else to do, other than hanging out in bars all the time. Don't get me wrong. I like my drink now and then, but it wears thin after a while. I mean, how many times can you get wasted before it gets old? A person needs something else, something...satisfying. Something that makes you feel good inside like—I don't know—wholesome? So I go visit my suit. Once a week I come down to the tailor shop. I try the suit on. I have it fitted. I visit with it, like if I was visiting with my relatives or something. The suit becomes family. I know it sounds screwy, but that's how I feel. It's gives me a place to go, you know?

KIMIYO: Why you not get wife, then no need suit?

SANTANA: Well, the suit is less complicated. Someday, when I retire from the corps, I'm gonna buy me a little house, and I'm gonna give my suits a home. They'll have their own rack to hang in.

KIMIYO: You not make sense, Santana-san.

SANTANA: So I'm a little nuts. What are you gonna do?

(KIMIYO *takes* SANTANA'*s other foot from the pan and begins to dry it.*)

SANTANA: Hey. You're finished already?

ACT ONE 19

KIMIYO: Feet clean now. Feel good?

SANTANA: Hmnnn. Feel very, very good.

KIMIYO: You like?

SANTANA: Yeah. Hmnnn. Your otosan gets this kind of treatment every night?

KIMIYO: Every night okasan wash.

SANTANA: He's a lucky guy, your father. What else does he get?

(KIMIYO *places the pan and towels back on the counter and then picks up one of the robes from the bed.*)

KIMIYO: Me, show. But first you put on yucata.

(KIMIYO *opens the robe for* SANTANA.)

SANTANA: Now?

KIMIYO: Must get ready. Sleep.

(SANTANA *tries to put the robe over his clothes.*)

KIMIYO: No-no-no! Must take off clothes first.

SANTANA: You want me to get undressed?

(KIMIYO *nods.*)

SANTANA: Hey. You sure you no waku-waku G I before?

KIMIYO: *(Shocked)* No!

SANTANA: All right, all right. I was just wondering.

KIMIYO: Kimiyo see ani and otosan and other shinseki before.

SANTANA: Your male relatives?

KIMIYO: Sometime see neighbor man also. See many, many man. But I no waku-waku like Santana-san say.

SANTANA: I believe you.

KIMIYO: Now put on yucata?

SANTANA: Okay, but I'm a little modest. *(He drapes the robe over his shoulders, turns his back to her, and removes his clothes.)*

KIMIYO: Kimiyo help.

SANTANA: Hold your horses. I can handle it.

(After removing his clothes, SANTANA secures the robe with the belt. He turns to KIMIYO.)

SANTANA: Ta-ta!

KIMIYO: *(Directing him to the chair)* Sit now.

(SANTANA sits. KIMIYO massages his shoulders.)

SANTANA: All right. Ahhh. Hey, you could make a lot of money doing this.

(KIMIYO stops and bows her head in shame.)

SANTANA: Hey, c'mon. What did I do?

KIMIYO: Kimiyo no do for money.

SANTANA: I didn't mean nothing. I was just paying you a compliment.

KIMIYO: Compliment?

SANTANA: Yeah. You know? Your massage is so good, it should be worth lots of money. I didn't mean anything else. I know you're a good girl.

KIMIYO: You like Kimiyo?

SANTANA: Sure, I like you. Any woman who is still a virgin at eighteen deserves a lot of respect. And I mean that. C'mon, keep doing my shoulders.

KIMIYO: *(Massaging his shoulders again)* You no respect number four geisha?

SANTANA: Sure. Why not? They gotta make a living, too. There's not much doing on this island except hooking or driving a taxi.

KIMIYO: What "hoo-king"?

ACT ONE

SANTANA: Prostitution. It's the only decent job here for a woman.

KIMIYO: No! Not decent. Very, very not decent.

SANTANA: I mean decent money. Hey, if I was a woman, I'd probably be hooking. That's why I can appreciate somebody like you who is willing to put in long hours in a tailor shop. You got principles. You make things happen on your own terms.

KIMIYO: Kimiyo do good work. Mama-san, papa-san, brothers, sisters all work. Make much money.

SANTANA: Doing what?

KIMIYO: Papa-san, brother fish big boat. Sell fish, make money. Mama-san, sisters—what you say? —saw?

SANTANA: Saw? You mean sew, like needle and thread sew?

KIMIYO: Yes. Sew clothes. *(She stops massaging him and walks to the bed.)*

SANTANA: That was great. I can let you do that for hours.

KIMIYO: Santana-san want more?

SANTANA: No, no. I'm fine.

KIMIYO: Get ready now. Go bed.

*(*SANTANA *lights up a cigarette and sits on the edge of the bed with his back to* KIMIYO. *She removes her clothes and slips into her yucata. He looks back and catches a glimpse of her naked body.)*

SANTANA: You…you can have the bed.

KIMIYO: Two sleep bed.

SANTANA: I don't think so. I'm not very sleepy.

KIMIYO: Santana-san no want sleep Kimiyo. Kimiyo sleep floor.

SANTANA: Look, I'm gonna be honest with you. When I first brought you up here, I had ideas. Not all the way from the beginning, but later, when you wouldn't go into any of the tea houses. Hey, I thought. Why not? I figured if you come up here, you had to know the score.

KIMIYO: No understand.

SANTANA: I'm trying to tell you is that I brought you up here to make love to you.

KIMIYO: Kimiyo understand.

SANTANA: No, you don't. A nice guy wouldn't have done that. But you're different, Kimiyo. I mean a real nice girl. And, well, it ain't right that something as important as...as giving yourself for the first time should be done in a hotel room with a guy like me. You deserve somebody special. And I ain't special.

(KIMIYO *sits on the opposite side of the bed with her back to* SANTANA.)

KIMIYO: Kimiyo think you special.

SANTANA: Nah. I'm just another jarhead. You stick your head out the window, and you see fifty like me. You gotta be a little more selective, or you'll end up on the street like those other girls.

KIMIYO: I like you.

SANTANA: You know nothing about me.

KIMIYO: I know much. You come tailor shop two months buy suit. I see you, and I think maybe you look at Kimiyo. But you no look. And all the time I think sometime you look and see Kimiyo and wanna take. No matter Kimiyo miss bus and no can go home. If parent no want Kimiyo, me not aflaid. Me wanna stay with you.

ACT ONE 23

SANTANA: Well, you can't, all right? I'm nobody. Nobody you should mess around with. In a couple of days, I'm gonna ship out. Gone-so, you know? No come back no more.

KIMIYO: Where you go?

SANTANA: Far away in a big ship.

KIMIYO: Amelica?

SANTANA: No.

KIMIYO: War? You go war?

SANTANA: What difference does it make?

KIMIYO: You go war? *(She starts to cry.)*

SANTANA: Hey, c'mon. What is this?

KIMIYO: You go war, you die. No see you no more.

SANTANA: It's what I've been trained to do. Your father catches fish. I fight for my country. It's a job like any other job.

KIMIYO: Only crazy man go war.

SANTANA: I'm a professional Marine. It's what I like to do. It makes me feel good. Just like working in a tailor shop make you feel good.

KIMIYO: I no like tailor shop.

SANTANA: Well, you know what I mean. Look, let's change the subject. I don't want to talk about it anymore.

KIMIYO: Your mother not worry?

SANTANA: I said, let's change the subject.

KIMIYO: Why you wanna die?

SANTANA: What is this with dying? *(He takes his jacket from the door and shows her his decorations.)* See these things? They're medals. You get them for doing a good job. I'm good at my job—one of the best. I don't plan on getting killed. So quit talking about dying, all right? I don't want to hear that kind of talk.

KIMIYO: Worthless girl make Santana-san angry.

SANTANA: Let's forget it. Why don't you get some sleep.

(A thunder peal cracks the serenity of the room.)

KIMIYO: *(Frightened)* Ahhh!...

SANTANA: It's just a thunder storm.

KIMIYO: Kamisama punish Kimiyo.

(The rain outside falls in torrents. SANTANA closes the window.)

SANTANA: Get some sleep. I'll be right here.

KIMIYO: *(Patting a spot next to her)* You come.

SANTANA: All right. I'll lie next to you. But you go to sleep, okay?

(SANTANA lies next to KIMIYO. After a moment, she nestles close to him. He turns down the lights. There is a warm glow in the room.)

SANTANA: Your mother is probably worried about you.

KIMIYO: Tomorrow I write her letter. Tell her Kimiyo never come home no more.

(The rain beats a steady, soothing patter throughout the remainder of the scene. Occasionally, a thunder clap punctuates the storm outside.)

SANTANA: You can't do that.

KIMIYO: Me can do. Think about long time.

SANTANA: Think about what, leaving?

KIMIYO: Yes. No go back home no more. Go to big country, Japan. Kimiyo be modern woman. Learn many things. Maybe go Tokyo. You go Tokyo, Santana-san?

ACT ONE 25

SANTANA: I've been there a couple of times.

KIMIYO: You like?

SANTANA: It's all right. Just another city.

KIMIYO: No, much beautiful. I see pictures in school. Big, big city. Lots more people. Maybe someday go aboard.

SANTANA: Aboard?

KIMIYO: Yes. Urope, Noway, Swissland, Fance. I see all big places, learn many things.

SANTANA: You have big dreams for a baby-san.

KIMIYO: No baby-san no more. Mother want Kimiyo marry. That make Kimiyo woman.

SANTANA: And you don't want to get married?

KIMIYO: Kimiyo want marry. But no want marry Okinawa man.

SANTANA: Why not?

KIMIYO: Okinawa man want Kimiyo stay in house and have many children. Take care old people. Kimiyo want to go big city like friend.

SANTANA: You have friend in Tokyo?

KIMIYO: Yes. School friend. Father sent her to number one college in Japan. She very smart and very rich. She writes of good life in Tokyo. She ask me go visit her.

SANTANA: Won't your honeywah be broken-hearted if you just dump him and go to Tokyo?

KIMIYO: What you mean dump?

SANTANA: Leave him. Break-off. No marry him. Him cry when you go Tokyo.

KIMIYO: No! —No! He no cry. He marry other woman.

SANTANA: But he loves you.

KIMIYO: He no love Kimiyo. He see picture and make business with father. Father say okay to marry Kimiyo. If I go Japan, he pick another picture of girl and marry same.

SANTANA: You've never met him?

KIMIYO: Never. Most Okinawa woman never know husband before marry. Father most time make business for husband.

SANTANA: So you meet your husband at the wedding ceremony?

KIMIYO: No. Meet before. Sometime two, three times. Then marry. You have wife?

SANTANA: No.

KIMIYO: Amelica honeywah?

SANTANA: Nope.

KIMIYO: You no like woman?

SANTANA: Sure, I like women. But there's nobody special.

KIMIYO: You like Okinawa woman?

SANTANA: A good Marine doesn't have time for women. You take them as they come along, but you don't marry them.

KIMIYO: Not get married?

SANTANA: We're on the go all the time. We don't have time to spend with a woman. Besides, you never know when you're going to buy it.

KIMIYO: Buy it?

SANTANA: Knocked off, you know, killed.

KIMIYO: Ahhh!...

SANTANA: I'm not saying it's gonna happen. But you never know.

ACT ONE

KIMIYO: Father go war. He say war very bad.

SANTANA: Second World War?

KIMIYO: He go China. Fight Chinese people.

SANTANA: Yeah? Did he ever kill anybody?

KIMIYO: He say Chinese people good people, like Japanese. All people same. All people think same. He say he kill no people only one pig.

SANTANA: Pig?

KIMIYO: Yes. Oink, oink, pig.

SANTANA: He was lucky.

KIMIYO: You kill people, Santana-san?

SANTANA: Go to sleep. It's late.

KIMIYO: No want sleep. Want talk.

SANTANA: Well, I'm tired of talking. C'mon. Try to sleep.

KIMIYO: I aflaid of tum-tum.

SANTANA: There's nothing to be afraid of.

KIMIYO: You no leave?

SANTANA: I won't leave. C'mon. Close your eyes.

(The lights dim lower. Suddenly, a peal of thunder frightens KIMIYO. *She stifles a scream.)*

SANTANA: It's okay. I'm here.

KIMIYO: Mother say, when thunder come Kamisama very angry.

SANTANA: Maybe He's got good reason to be angry.

KIMIYO: I very aflaid, Santana-san.

SANTANA: Don't be. If God's angry at anyone, it isn't you. I don't think anyone can be angry at you. Now close your eyes. Sleep. You're safe here.

KIMIYO: You stay close, okay?

SANTANA: I'm here.

(KIMIYO *nestles close to* SANTANA. *There's a momentary silence except for the steady drone of the rain.*)

KIMIYO: Santana-san?

SANTANA: Yeah.

KIMIYO: Why you not go home?

SANTANA: Home?

KIMIYO: Yes. Amelica. Like other G I.

SANTANA: The Marine Corps is my home.

KIMIYO: No. Maline Ko not home. Go home to mother-san, papa-san.

SANTANA: I don't have a mother-san.

KIMIYO: No? No have mother-san?

SANTANA: No.

KIMIYO: She die?

SANTANA: I don't know. Maybe. I never knew her.

KIMIYO: Not know mother-san? Why not?

SANTANA: I never got a chance to meet her. I never met my father either. I don't know nobody. All she left me was a piece of paper with a name, a religion, and two words. Words I've never been able to understand.

KIMIYO: Words?

SANTANA: Yeah. Puerto Rican. You ever hear of them?

KIMIYO: No.

SANTANA: Well, then, you know as much about them as I do.

KIMIYO: What mean words?

ACT ONE

SANTANA: I told you, I don't know. I thought I did once, but I was wrong.

KIMIYO: I have book. Maybe you find words in book, dik-sio-nary.

SANTANA: No. Not these words. You won't find them in the dictionary, not what they really mean. Hell, there was a time when I thought I knew what they meant. I put them on like you put on a new suit. And they seemed to fit too. I strutted around with them words on me. It was a good feeling. *(Suddenly remembering something)* I wish to hell she'd never written them on that piece of paper.

KIMIYO: Why not?

SANTANA: Because I'm a Marine. As long as I got that uniform on, people know who I am. They don't care if I'm Puerto Rican, Irish, or anything else. I'm a man, and they know that. And that's all that counts.

KIMIYO: You Amelica man, yes?

SANTANA: Yeah, I guess. Let me tell you something, Kimiyo. You're Okinawan, pure bred, right through to your toes. You know who and what you are, and that's important. Especially in America. They make a big deal about it over there. People go around patting themselves in the back about what they are. Hell, they even got parades to let people know. It's like nobody wants to come from there. You'd fit right in with them. Why, if you get enough Okinawans over there, you could have your own parade.

KIMIYO: They got parade for you, Santana-san?

SANTANA: No. They don't have parades for nobodies. And that's what you are when you can't claim to be from someplace, a nobody. I know. I tried to fit in once.

KIMIYO: Fit in?

SANTANA: Yeah. Try to belong somewhere. Be part of something, like a team. I tried to be a Puerto Rican, but I didn't know what it was all about. It's something you don't learn. Either you're born into it, or you're not.

KIMIYO: Not understand, Santana-san.

SANTANA: Look, I was dumped in an orphanage when I was a baby, maybe a few weeks old. They don't teach you anything there. They give you food, clothes, a place to sleep. But that's all. You can't learn there what you were meant to be. Like in your case, you're an Okinawan. Well, you could only learn that from your mother, your father, and from living here.

KIMIYO: Ahh!...

SANTANA: But one thing you do learn in the States is that you gotta be from somewhere. 'Cause the minute you walk on the streets, somebody is gonna ask you what you are. And if you say you're an American, they're gonna come back with "Yeah, I know that, but what are you? Where are you from? Where do your parents come from?" They got words like roots and heritage, and they tell you how you gotta be proud of them, proud of where your parents came from. It's not enough that you're an American. You gotta be from someplace else. And when you come from an orphanage, you're from nowhere. *(Pause)* I remember when I was a kid in the orphanage. We would divvy up into groups. The black kids would go around braiding their hair and calling themselves Africans. And we'd go around jiving and walking with our backs hunched, slapping each other in the hands 'cause that was the way Puerto Ricans acted on the streets and in the movies. What did we know? We just copied everything people said was Puerto Rican. Until one day—when I was eighteen—I went to Puerto Rico and found out that I wasn't Puerto Rican at all. When

ACT ONE

I went into my Puerto Rican act there, they laughed. They called me an Americano. Me, who was trying so hard to be like them. They couldn't even understand my Spanish. They just laughed. Laughed as if I were a clown.

KIMIYO: Not worry, Santana-san

SANTANA: That's when I realized I didn't belong. So I stopped being a Puerto Rican and joined the Marine Corps. They gave me a uniform, and nobody cared what I was 'cause I was a Marine, and that's something. And that's what I am. So you see, I have no need of those words anymore.

KIMIYO: Words make you sad. Very, very sad.

SANTANA: Nah. Not anymore. That's old stuff. I don't even know why I brought it up. C'mon. Let's try to get some shut-eye.

KIMIYO: Not can sleep. Room very cold.

SANTANA: Here. Keep this over yourself.

(SANTANA *tucks* KIMIYO *in. She places his arm around her and snuggles into it.*)

KIMIYO: Much better now. *(A long pause)* Santana-san?

SANTANA: What?

KIMIYO: I not afraid leave Okinawa…I not afraid be nobody like you.

(KIMIYO *and* SANTANA *huddle together as the hypnotic patter of the rain fills the room. The lights fade slowly to black.*)

END OF ACT ONE

ACT TWO

Scene One

(Later that night. KIMIYO *and* SANTANA *are asleep. The room is illuminated by an occasional burst of lightning.)*

(Imperceptible at first, the sounds of rain and thunder gradually change into the sounds of gunfire and exploding mortar shells. KIMIYO *is still in sleep while* SANTANA *tosses in a troubled sleep.)*

(In the darkness, we hear the urgent shouts of Viet Cong soldiers together with SANTANA*'s and* KELLER*'s desperate voices. The mix creates a surrealistic cacophony of horror that is accentuated by blinding flashes of light.)*

KELLER'S VOICE: Hey, Joe, you still there? Joe. Joe!

SANTANA: Shut up, Keller!

KELLER'S VOICE: They're getting close, Joe.

SANTANA: Shut your fucking mouth! They're gonna get a fix on us.

VIET CONG VOICE #1: We know you there, America. You come out.

VIET CONG VOICE #2: Throw out gun—give up!

KELLER'S VOICE: They're all around us, Joe.

SANTANA: Canned it. You're gonna give away our positions.

VIET CONG VOICE #1: Last chance, America. Soon all die.

KELLER'S VOICE: Joe, they're crawling all over the place. I'm coming in.

SANTANA: Don't, man. Don't! I can't see a fucking thing!

KELLER'S VOICE: I'm coming in, Joe.

(Sounds of crawling bodies are heard.)

VIET CONG VOICE #2: Here's grenade for you, Joe.

(A light flashes and a thunderous explosion goes off. SANTANA, startled, sits up in bed in firing position. We hear the rattle of his automatic rifle.)

SANTANA: *(Reliving the experience)* C'mon, you sonavabitches! C'mon!

(KIMIYO jumps out of bed in terror. She turns on the lights. The war sounds are replaced by the soothing sound of the falling rain. SANTANA sits in bed, still clutching his imaginary M-14. His body is soaked in sweat. She climbs back into bed and tries to awaken him.)

KIMIYO: Santana-san. Santana-san!

SANTANA: *(Shakes uncontrollably.)* They're all around us… They're coming in!

KIMIYO: Santana-san! You must wake up!

(KIMIYO shakes him. He snaps out of it and looks up at her surprisedly.)

KIMIYO: Bad dream. Bad dream. *(She feels the intense heat of his body.)* You sick, Santana-san. You very, very hot.

(SANTANA shivers. KIMIYO goes to the sink and fills a pan with water. She applies a cold towel to his face.)

SANTANA: *(In delirium)* Keller? …Keller!

ACT TWO

KIMIYO: *(Soothingly)* Dream all gone now. All gone.

SANTANA: Have you seen Keller? Have you seen him?

(KIMIYO *eases* SANTANA *out of his robe and gasps at seeing the scars on his body.*)

KIMIYO: Oh! ...What happen! Santana-san!

SANTANA: They're dead. They're all dead...

KIMIYO: Your chest! Agh!

SANTANA: There was no other way. I had to do it...

(KIMIYO *shakes him violently.*)

KIMIYO: You wake, yes! You wake!

(SANTANA *grabs* KIMIYO *in his delirium and shakes her.*)

SANTANA: You believe me, don't you? You believe me!

(KIMIYO *screams and snaps* SANTANA *out of his delirium.*)

SANTANA: What's going on? What happened?

KIMIYO: No hurt, please. No hurt.

SANTANA: Hurt?

(SANTANA *notices that he's holding* KIMIYO. *He pulls his hands away. She jumps to the middle of the room.*)

SANTANA: *(Continuing)* I'm sorry if I hurt you.

KIMIYO: You crazy man.

SANTANA: I must've been dreaming...

(*As* SANTANA *sits up, we can see three deep gashes across his chest and two smaller ones on his right shoulder. A colorful tattoo of a bulldog adorns his right forearm. He reaches out for* KIMIYO, *but she draws back.*)

KIMIYO: No! Please.

SANTANA: I'm not going to hurt you.

(SANTANA *reaches for* KIMIYO *again and collapses on the floor. He is too weak to stand.*)

KIMIYO: No. You no touch, okay? *(She tries to sneak past him.)* No touch.

SANTANA: Don't be afraid. I'm okay now.

KIMIYO: You very, very crazy.

SANTANA: It's just the fever.

KIMIYO: Fever?

SANTANA: It makes Santana dream funny. You get me pills from jacket.

KIMIYO: Pills?

SANTANA: In my jacket, there's some pills. You get, and then I feel better. No more fever.

KIMIYO: You no grab, Kimiyo?

SANTANA: No.

(KIMIYO goes around SANTANA to the hanging jacket.)

SANTANA: In the breast pocket.

(KIMIYO pulls out a silver packet from the jacket pocket.)

SANTANA: That's it. And a glass of water, please.

(KIMIYO pours SANTANA a glass of water and cautiously hands him the water and the pills.)

SANTANA: Thanks.

(SANTANA opens the packet, pops the pills into his mouth, and washes them down with the water. KIMIYO stands by the bed watching him.)

KIMIYO: You better now?

SANTANA: Yeah. Can you throw me the blanket?

(KIMIYO pulls the blanket off the bed and throws it to SANTANA. He drapes it over his shivering body.)

KIMIYO: You should go hospital.

SANTANA: I'll be all right in a few minutes.

ACT TWO

KIMIYO: Who Kerer, Santana-san?

SANTANA: Who?

KIMIYO: You yell, "Kerer! Kerer!" like crazy man.

SANTANA: What else did I say?

KIMIYO: I not know. Maybe you lose Kerer. You say, "Where Kerer?" I not know Kerer. Ah, yes. You say, "All dead."

SANTANA: Dead?

KIMIYO: Yes, dead. Who dead, Santana-san?

SANTANA: I'm cold. Can you hand me another blanket?

(KIMIYO *pulls the sheet off the bed and wraps it around* SANTANA.)

KIMIYO: Better?

(SANTANA *nods.* KIMIYO *goes to the table and pours him the last of the tea. He tries to hold the cup, but his hands are shaking badly. She puts the cup to his lips.*)

KIMIYO: Tea good. You drink all.

(SANTANA *drains the cup.* KIMIYO *takes the cup from him and rubs his arms to warm him.*)

KIMIYO: Why you have so many cuts on body? Marine Ko?

SANTANA: No. Viet Cong.

KIMIYO: Ah, war. Not hurt?

SANTANA: Nah. It's all healed.

KIMIYO: What picture in arm mean?

SANTANA: The tattoo? It's the Marine Corps mascot, a bulldog.

KIMIYO: Bulldog?

SANTANA: A ferocious dog, like Marines. Big fighter. Never gives up.

KIMIYO: You never give up?

SANTANA: Never! A Marine fights to the end.

KIMIYO: Why?

SANTANA: 'Cause he does, that's why. We don't take no bull-crap from nobody.

KIMIYO: Better to live, no?

SANTANA: What's the difference? One day is pretty much like the other, isn't it?

KIMIYO: No. Every day different.

SANTANA: Not to me it ain't.

KIMIYO: You don't want live?

SANTANA: Sure, I wanna live. But if I die, I die. I'm not gonna worry about it.

KIMIYO: Me worry.

SANTANA: Why?

KIMIYO: Not want die. Want to live. Go to Tokyo, aboard. Maybe go Amelica someday. See wonderful things. Enjoy. No can do if Kimiyo dead. When dead, no can do nothing.

SANTANA: Don't kid yourself, it's all the same, different faces, different languages, but the same people. Nothing changes. You're better off at home with you family, at least, they care about you. That's the best you can hope for in this world.

KIMIYO: No. Hope for many things. I want marry, have children, have good husband that let Kimiyo learn be modern woman.

SANTANA: Good luck.

KIMIYO: You not want marry?

SANTANA: I'm married to the corps. No woman is gonna want me.

ACT TWO

KIMIYO: I want.

(SANTANA *looks at* KIMIYO *suspiciously.*)

SANTANA: What do you want with a guy like me?

KIMIYO: You need good woman take care of you.

SANTANA: I can take care of myself.

KIMIYO: You no get lonesome?

SANTANA: No. I don't.

KIMIYO: I no believe.

SANTANA: What do you mean, you don't believe? What do you know about it?

KIMIYO: Kimiyo see you cry. You very, very aflaid.

SANTANA: Afraid? Me? I ain't afraid of nothing. When did I cry?

KIMIYO: When you have bad dream.

SANTANA: Hey, I couldn't help that. I was delirious. People do crazy things when they're delirious.

KIMIYO: Why you cry?

SANTANA: Lay-off, will ya? Is there any more of that tea?

KIMIYO: Tea all gone.

SANTANA: Get me the sake then.

KIMIYO: No. Sake very bad for you. You sick.

SANTANA: I'm not sick anymore. I just have some kinks in my back, that's all. Get me the bottle.

KIMIYO: No need sake. Kimiyo make you feel better.

SANTANA: I want a drink.

KIMIYO: No. You lie on floor.

(SANTANA *sees the determination on* KIMIYO's *face.*)

KIMIYO: You do.

SANTANA: What are you gonna do?

KIMIYO: Lie stomach.

(SANTANA *lies on his stomach.* KIMIYO *removes his coverings.*)

SANTANA: What are you doing?

KIMIYO: Make body relax.

(KIMIYO *kneels beside* SANTANA *and gently massages his back.*)

SANTANA: Is that what you people do all the time, massage each other?

KIMIYO: You no like?

SANTANA: Sure. But it ain't gonna cure all the ills of the world.

KIMIYO: Father-san say body must be at peace before mind can find wisdom.

SANTANA: He sounds like a wise man.

KIMIYO: Sometime. Other time, not so wise.

SANTANA: Do you like him?

KIMIYO: Very much. Him good provider and husband.

SANTANA: Is that all a man has to do to be liked?

KIMIYO: Must have good heart.

SANTANA: And he has a good heart.

KIMIYO: Yes. Maybe heart too good. Make mother strong. *(She giggles.)*

SANTANA: He's henpecked?

KIMIYO: What henpeck?

SANTANA: He's under your mother's thumb. She controls him.

ACT TWO

KIMIYO: No! Father big boss in house…sometime. But mother sometime stubborn. Must have way. Much talk until father say okay.

SANTANA: Looks like you take after your mother, the way you've been bossing me around.

KIMIYO: No! Kimiyo not want tell people what to do. All people free. Do what they want.

SANTANA: Is that what you want? To be free?

KIMIYO: Already free. Not go home no more.

SANTANA: Yeah? Well, wait until you've been on your own for awhile. Then maybe you won't want to be so free. It's pretty rough out there when you're all alone.

KIMIYO: You strong now, Santana-san?

SANTANA: Yeah. That massage is doing the job.

(KIMIYO *stands.*)

SANTANA: Hey, don't stop now.

KIMIYO: I stand on your back. Make you feel much better.

SANTANA: Stand on me?

KIMIYO: Mother stand on father. Father like very much. Make you feel more relax.

SANTANA: Yeah?

KIMIYO: You strong. Hold Kimiyo?

SANTANA: Yeah, sure. Climb on. We'll give it a shot.

(KIMIYO *stands barefooted on* SANTANA's *back.*)

KIMIYO: Kimiyo not too heavy?

SANTANA: Nah. You're as light as a feather.

KIMIYO: I walk now.

(KIMIYO *moves carefully on* SANTANA's *back, kneading his back muscles with her feet.*)

KIMIYO: Feel good?

SANTANA: Yeah. Great.

(KIMIYO *continues to work* SANTANA's *back.*)

KIMIYO: You think Kimiyo speak good English?

SANTANA: Very good.

KIMIYO: Work very hard learn English. Maybe become translator, do you think?

SANTANA: Translator?

KIMIYO: Yes. They need translator in Japan, yes?

SANTANA: I don't know. Maybe.

KIMIYO: You think Kimiyo get job?

SANTANA: Are you really serious about going there?

KIMIYO: Very serious. Want new life.

SANTANA: But you're just a kid. Aren't you afraid of going to such a big place by yourself.

KIMIYO: Why aflaid?

(KIMIYO *steps off and sits pensively on* SANTANA's *buttocks.*)

SANTANA: What if you don't find work? What are you gonna do then?

KIMIYO: Kimiyo find.

SANTANA: But what if you don't? How are you going to live? You need a place to stay. You need food, clothes...

(KIMIYO *stands on* SANTANA *again.*)

KIMIYO: Must think positive. (*She digs her feet angrily into his back.*) I want be modern woman. If I must take chance, then I will take chance. Otherwise, stay here and be like sister. That not very good.

SANTANA: Okay, look. Get off me for a minute.

ACT TWO

(KIMIYO *steps off.*)

SANTANA: There's a little matter of money. Have you got some yen stashed away, dollars?

KIMIYO: No. No have money.

SANTANA: You plan to go back to the tailor shop and make some?

KIMIYO: No! Not go back to uncle's shop.

SANTANA: All right, then, where is the money gonna come from?

KIMIYO: Not know.

SANTANA: Then don't you think you should go back home until you think this out more?

KIMIYO: No. Not go home. Must do now.

SANTANA: There's no way you're gonna do it right now. A major move like that has gotta be planned out, and you got no plans—nothing.

(KIMIYO *stands. She picks up one of the sheets from the floor and takes it to bed.*)

SANTANA: Whatta you doing?

KIMIYO: Go to bed now, sleep. Must think of what to do.

SANTANA: Don't go to sleep now. Stay up. We'll talk a little bit. We'll talk about other things. What do you want to talk about?

KIMIYO: Not want talk anymore. I must plan what to do. In morning, I must have plan.

SANTANA: C'mon. Stay up. (*He looks at his watch.*) It's three-thirty in the morning. C'mon. I don't want to sleep.

KIMIYO: No. Must sleep. I no can think when you talk.

SANTANA: Then we won't talk. We'll just sit here.

KIMIYO: No want sit.

(KIMIYO *gets in bed and pulls the sheet over her.* SANTANA *sits on the bed.*)

SANTANA: Please don't go to sleep, Kimiyo. Please? I don't wanna be by myself.

KIMIYO: Why? You say you like being by self. Not need anyone.

SANTANA: I lied.

KIMIYO: Lied?

SANTANA: I can't sleep at night. If I go to sleep, I'll have the same dream again.

KIMIYO: Bad dream?

SANTANA: Yeah. Unless I get plastered, then I don't dream of nothing. I just conk out.

KIMIYO: Conk out?

SANTANA: Pass out, you know? From booze.

KIMIYO: What is dream?

SANTANA: It's a mess. Too complicated to talk about.

KIMIYO: Then I go sleep.

SANTANA: I can't talk about it. Don't you understand? It's personal.

KIMIYO: Mother say, when bad dream come, person must talk about dream. Then bad dream not come back.

SANTANA: Not this one.

KIMIYO: You talk. I listen.

SANTANA: I can't… I just can't.

KIMIYO: Why not?

SANTANA: I don't know. I just can't. I ain't never told nobody.

ACT TWO

KIMIYO: You want dream go away?

SANTANA: Yeah. If only it could.

KIMIYO: Then you talk.

SANTANA: Do you think it will really go away?

KIMIYO: Yes.

SANTANA: I gotta have a drink first, though. *(He goes to the table, pours himself a cup of sake, and gulps it.)* You won't tell nobody? Yeah, right. Who you gonna tell. First, you gotta understand that I'm a good Marine, as good as anybody. I went through boot camp, seen some action, and I've done the job when I had to. I've even been decorated a few times. So I ain't no slouch, you know? It's important you know that 'cause I don't want you to think I'm some candy ass, or something. I'm as tough as any of them. But you know, when they first sent me over to Viet Nam, I was just a boot, fresh out of basic training. I didn't know anything. I had less than a year in. Anyway, we're out in the field and the C O says he's got reports of enemy activity a few miles north of our camp. Sergeant Hines asked for volunteers to check out the area. So me and two other guys, who were on latrine duty, volunteered. What did we know? We figured it'd be easy duty. Anything was better than digging trenches for latrines. Anyhow, the three of us and the sergeant set out to reconnoiter the situation. When we got about a half mile from the camp, all hell broke loose. *(He pauses.)* Bullets were flying from everywhere. The sergeant got it first, right in the side of the face. Then Milks got it. Well, I just started running. I ran right into the bush. This other guy, Keller, was right behind me. We didn't know where to go, so we stayed put, hoping they wouldn't come after us. We were scared shit the two of us. *(He looks at her questioningly.)* I mean, it wasn't supposed to be that way. They weren't supposed to be there.

They were supposed to be miles up north. But there they were, all over the place. I figured that was it. It was over. I had never seen anybody get killed before. And all of a sudden, two of my friends are dead, and we're next. Keller knew it too. He kept looking at me with big eyes, wondering what we were gonna do to stop it. The sun was going down, so we dug in. We dug and dug into that ground until we couldn't dig no more. I kept hoping our guys had heard the shots and that they come to help us. But nobody came. It was just the two of us in that jungle, in the dark. We couldn't even see our hands in front of our face it was so black. *(Beat)* And then they started. "Hey, America, give up. You gonna die." That kinda stuff. I never prayed before, but I was praying that night. I remembered what they use to tell us at boot camp. How we had to be tough. How no Marine ever gave up... Well, I never figured it was gonna be like that. Alone and scared in the middle of nowhere with the mosquitoes eating your eyes out. I didn't wanna die, not there, not then. It wasn't fair. I hadn't lived yet. I was nineteen years old. I hadn't done or seen anything. Nobody knew who I was. And if I died, nobody would know I ever existed. *(He lets out a rueful laugh.)* There wouldn't even be a place to send the body. I thought of giving up. But then I remembered what they taught us at I T R. Recon patrols don't take prisoners. And those guys weren't about to take any. So I just lay there in the hole I had dug and died. Every time I'd hear a branch crack or a bush rustle, I'd die. I died a thousand times that night. Then Keller started calling out to me. At first, he just wanted to make sure I hadn't run out on him. I told him to keep quiet, but he was scared too, I guess. Every once in a while he'd call. And then the V. C. picked up on it and started calling me by name. "Hey, Santana, why you wanna die?" They kept it going all night. At least until I dozed off. Then I heard it. The

ACT TWO

crawling. Bodies scraping against the ground. They were close, real close. I grabbed my rifle and aimed it at the noise and fired. I couldn't see them, but I could hear their screams as the bullets would find them. I fired at the flash of their rifles. I fired at everything until I had nothing left. Then I leaned back against the wall of the hole and waited for them. *(He wipes at his tears.)* I waited until I saw the first light come through the trees. Then I heard the footsteps, a lot of them. This figure stepped at the edge of my hole, and I closed my eyes and waited for it to come. But it didn't come. Instead I heard my name, "Hey, Santana. Are you all right?" I opened my eyes, and there was Corporal Bridges looking down at me. He helped me out of the foxhole, and then I saw what I had done. *(He begins to sob.)* It was Keller. He was right next to my hole dead, bullet holes all over him. I didn't know he was out there. I never heard him. He was just lying there with his head shot off.

KIMIYO: You all right, Santana-san?

SANTANA: He shouldn't have come out of his hole...He shouldn't have come out of his hole.

KIMIYO: Not your fault, Santana-san. Not your fault.

SANTANA: How was I supposed to know he was out there? They were coming for me.

KIMIYO: Person do strange thing when frightened. Sometime not good thing, but must understand reason. Very important understand reason.

SANTANA: It was basic. You don't leave your hole under those conditions. Any boot knows that.

KIMIYO: Bad mistake. That is all.

SANTANA: He had no business being out there, Kimiyo. No business at all.

(KIMIYO *strokes* SANTANA's *hair.*)

KIMIYO: You think him enemy. You frightened.

SANTANA: No! Marines are not supposed to be frightened. We're trained against it. We're not supposed to crack.

KIMIYO: Only so much person can do, Santana-san. Father frightened too when he go China, fight Chinese people. He say he very frightened. All people frightened sometime. Not lose face. Maybe you not kill friend. Maybe enemy people kill Kerer.

SANTANA: I killed him. I'm sure, I killed him.

KIMIYO: What you do now, Santana-san? You not want to understand reason.

SANTANA: Reason?

KIMIYO: Reason Kerer die. You must understand reason.

(SANTANA *gives* KIMIYO *a long look, then sits defeatedly at the edge of the bed.*)

SANTANA: He died because I broke under pressure. I lost control and fired into the darkness. He's dead because I'm a coward.

KIMIYO: You not coward. You very brave. Have medals.

SANTANA: *(Incongruously)* Medals? ...Medals? *(He laughs ironically.)* Do you know that they gave me a medal for it. I killed my buddy, and they gave me a medal. They said it was for valor against great odds. Valor. I aimed my M-14 into the night and fired. That's all I did. I was shitting in my pants and I fired at anything and everything that made a sound. I would have killed every man in my company if they had been out there that night. That's how brave I was. And you know, when they gave me the medal, I was too much of a coward to tell them what I had done. Funny, isn't

ACT TWO

it? They gave me a medal for cowardice. I keep forcing myself out there hoping that somehow—by some miracle—I won't be scared anymore. But each time is worse than the last. I don't know how long I can keep faking it. Maybe, maybe if I get it…

KIMIYO: No! You not say that, Santana-san.

SANTANA: If I'm dead, I won't have to deal with it anymore.

KIMIYO: If you dead, not bring Kerer back. And you not enter place of honorable spirits. Spirit must be calm in world of living, or not be able rest in world of dead. Father-san say, brave man foolish man. He say fear is friend of living. You make friend of fear, Santana-san, yes? Then fear not let you die. You must accept.

SANTANA: That I'm a coward?

KIMIYO: That you are aflaid to die. There is no shame in such fear. Old Okinawa saying, "When you travel with current of river, voyage require no effort". Maybe you run with current, yes?

SANTANA: But it ain't manly to run. A man has got to have something to believe in. All I've got is my pride. If I lose that, I've got nothing.

KIMIYO: Pride not good for dead person. Once dead, nobody remembers. Father's brothers all dead. Die in old war. All very proud. Now only father remember brothers. He wish brothers not so proud. Live brothers better. You must not be so proud, Santana-san.

SANTANA: I wish I could be like you. You're strong. Nothing can put you down. You can take anything and turn it around and make it work for you. I can't do that.

KIMIYO: You are good, young. Very brave. But not have someone. All persons need someone. Then things not so bad.

SANTANA: I don't know. I don't know what it's like to have someone. I never had nobody. But what about you? You don't need anybody. You're running away from those who love you. Your family.

KIMIYO: Kimiyo not run from family. Run from old life to new life. Run from mother's wishes.

SANTANA: But what about them? You'll break their hearts.

KIMIYO: Family very traditional. If I stay home and not follow parent's advice, then they lose face with neighbors. Better I go, send letter to mother. Then come back another time when all is past. Maybe then parents forgive Kimiyo.

SANTANA: It take guts to do what you're doing.

KIMIYO: Kimiyo not have guts. Very frightened. But must do what mind say. *(Her voice softens.)* Why you not come with me, Santana-san? Then I give you family you not have.

SANTANA: You mean go over the hill? Desert?

KIMIYO: We go Japan. Nobody find. Then we together.

SANTANA: I can't do that.

KIMIYO: Then I speak with Kamisama, ask not let anything bad happen to you.

SANTANA: I wish I could do that, Kimiyo. I really do.

KIMIYO: You must not make wish if heart not want wish.

(SANTANA *takes* KIMIYO's *arm.*)

SANTANA: My heart wants it very much. You're a wonderful person.

KIMIYO: Kimiyo not yet wonderful. But maybe soon. Then Santana-san find she worthy of praise.

ACT TWO

SANTANA: I can think of no praise that would be worthy of you.

(KIMIYO *and* SANTANA *look longingly at each other.*)

KIMIYO: Does Santana-san wish to kiss me?

SANTANA: Very much.

(SANTANA *kisses* KIMIYO *gently on the lips.*)

KIMIYO: Thank you for wonderful kiss. Maybe we do again, yes?

(SANTANA *kisses* KIMIYO *gently at first. She puts her arms around his neck and returns his kiss with fervor.*)

KIMIYO: Kiss better than imagination.

SANTANA: You've never kissed a man before?

KIMIYO: No. Not like this. It is very pleasant, isn't it?

SANTANA: Yes, it is.

(KIMIYO *and* SANTANA *kiss again.*)

SANTANA: Maybe we should stop.

KIMIYO: You not like?

SANTANA: I like very much. But if we keep doing it, I don't know if I can stop myself.

(KIMIYO *looks lovingly into* SANTANA*'s eyes.*)

KIMIYO: Why you wish to stop self, Santana-san? Not better let feelings flow with river?

(SANTANA *kisses* KIMIYO *softly over her face. She removes her robe and lies back on the bed. He places himself over her.*)

SANTANA: I, I think I love you.

KIMIYO: Yes. That is a wonderful wish.

(KIMIYO *and* SANTANA *embrace as the lights fade slowly. The lulling sound of the falling rain fills the room.*)

(*End of scene*)

Scene Two

(Later that night. KIMIYO *and* SANTANA *are in bed asleep. The rainstorm outside rages. He slips quietly out of bed and looks for his clothes.)*

(As SANTANA *stealthily collects his clothes, flashes of lightning illuminate him.)*

*(*SANTANA *dresses quickly, takes a last look at the sleeping figure of* KIMIYO, *and steals out the door.)*

(End of scene)

Scene Three

(The first morning light filters through the window. KIMIYO *turns in her sleep and with an errant hand reaches for the missing* SANTANA. *After a few exploratory stabs, her eyes snap open, and she jumps to a sitting position.)*

KIMIYO: Santana!... *(Her eyes quickly survey the room. When she finally accepts that he is gone, she slips out from under the covers and sits at the edge of the bed.)*

(After a moment, KIMIYO *lets out a soft sob. She drags herself to her feet and begins the arduous task of dressing. When she is dressed, she meticulously goes about the business of straightening the room.)*

(Just as KIMIYO *finishes making the bed,* SANTANA *appears at the door. He is carrying a rectangular, gift-wrapped box under his arm. She stares at him as if he were an apparition.)*

KIMIYO: Santana-san!

*(*KIMIYO *runs to* SANTANA *and throws herself at him, crying.)*

KIMIYO: I so aflaid...I so aflaid I not see you again.

*(*SANTANA *is visibly affected by* KIMIYO's *burst of emotion. He rocks her in his arms comfortingly.)*

ACT TWO

SANTANA: It's okay. I just wanted to get you something.

(KIMIYO *clings desperately to* SANTNA.)

SANTANA: Don't you want to see what it is?

KIMIYO: *(Still holding on to him)* Yes.

(SANTANA *shows* KIMIYO *the box, but she makes no attempt for it.*)

SANTANA: Well?

KIMIYO: Why you go and not tell me?

SANTANA: I wanted to surprise you.

KIMIYO: Kimiyo not like surprise. You not surprise me no more, okay?

SANTANA: I'm sorry. I thought I'd be back before you woke up.

KIMIYO: Not do that. I very, very aflaid. Have terrible dream.

SANTANA: You had a nightmare?

KIMIYO: End of dream, very, very bad.

SANTANA: Tell me about it.

(SANTANA *edges his way to the bed with* KIMIYO *still attached to him. He throws the package on the bed.*)

KIMIYO: Too terrible to tell. Want hold you longer.

SANTANA: C'mon. Sit down. Remember what mama-san said. If you talk about dream, it won't come back.

(KIMIYO *releases her hold on* SANTANA *and sits.*)

KIMIYO: First part, not so bad. Last part, very, very bad.

SANTANA: Then tell me the first part.

KIMIYO: First part Kimiyo and Santana-san walk long, long road. Hold hands very happy. But maybe Kimiyo mitsu-mitsu happy. In heart feel happy but lonesome.

Feel much love but love make Kimiyo lonesome. Make sense, Santana-san?

SANTANA: I think so.

KIMIYO: We walk, hold hands on road. But nothing on road, just long road. Then come to last part. At end of road, big intersection with many roads and old lady selling many kind pots.

SANTANA: Yeah.

KIMIYO: All pots on blanket on middle of street. Many kind pots: tea pot, coffee pot, even electric toaster. So Santana and Kimiyo kneel on street to look at pots. Old lady say, "Want go business?" And I say, we must take all pots and electric toaster to make business. You take coffee pot in hand and say, we need only coffee pot to open business. I say, sell only coffee pot not so good. Not many people buy coffee pot. Not can make living with only coffee pot. Then I talk to old lady to make business. And when I finish talking to old lady, I look to you, but you not there. Only empty road. Then I feel bad. I run empty streets look for you but not can find. Then heart feel very, very lonesome. I want find you, tell you okay. We not need other pots. I want tell you okay to open coffee pot business only.

SANTANA: Is that it?

KIMIYO: Yes.

SANTANA: That wasn't such a bad dream.

KIMIYO: Very bad dream. Kimiyo not find Santana-san. Kimiyo want tell Santana-san okay buy coffee pot. *(She begins to cry.)* You want buy coffee pot, Santana-san? You buy.

SANTANA: You were right. We can't make a business on just coffee pots. I'm a lousy business man.

KIMIYO: I'm sorry.

ACT TWO

SANTANA: It was only a dream.

KIMIYO: All very real.

SANTANA: I know.

(KIMIYO *wipes her tears.*)

KIMIYO: Why you come back, Santana-san?

SANTANA: I don't know. I wanted to get you something. Something special. But all the stores are closed. I went back to the base and looked through my things, and I discovered that I don't have anything. Nothing that's worth anything, except maybe what's in the box. It's all that I have to give you...I love you, Kimiyo. I'll love you forever.

(KIMIYO *and* SANTANA *embrace lovingly.*)

SANTANA: I know G Is always say they'll come back, but I want to come back. I want to come back to you.

KIMIYO: Then come back, Santana-san. I will wait for you.

SANTANA: But what about your dream?

KIMIYO: *(Touching her heart)* Dream right here with you. When you come back, we make dream come true...together. I go home now and make mother-san understand.

SANTANA: Home?

KIMIYO: Yes. Kimiyo face music like Santana-san say.

SANTANA: But you said you couldn't go home anymore. You'd lose face.

KIMIYO: Yesterday, I school child—must listen to mother. Now not child no more. I must do what is in heart, Santana-san. I not aflaid to lose face.

SANTANA: But what if your mother doesn't understand? What will you do then?

KIMIYO: Not worry. I tell mama-san, Kimiyo woman now. Not need picture husband. Find own man. She understand. You go. Come back. I wait, Santana-san. I wait for you.

(KIMIYO *and* SANTANA *hold each other for moment.*)

KIMIYO: You go now, please. You go before you see the foolishness of a child.

(SANTANA *goes to the door, turns, and exits.*)

(*After a long moment,* KIMIYO *goes to the bed, looks at the box, and opens it. She pulls out* SANTANA*'s grey suit. She holds it close to her.*)

(*The lights fade slowly to black.*)

END OF PLAY

www.ingramcontent.com/pod-product-compliance
Lightning Source LLC
Chambersburg PA
CBHW072016060426
42446CB00043B/2575